T0304461

ANIMAL AFTERLIFE

OTHER TITLES FROM AIRLIE PRESS

animal
afterlife

Poems

JAYA STENQUIST

WINNER OF THE
AIRLIE PRIZE

2022

Airlie Press is supported by book sales,
by contributions to the press from its
supporters, and by the work donated
by all the poet-editors of the press.

P.O. Box 13325
Portland OR 97213
www.airliepress.org
email: airliepress@gmail.com

**CLEAN
WATER
LAND &
LEGACY**
AMENDMENT

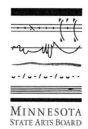

MINNESOTA
STATE ARTS BOARD

First Edition
ISBN 978-1-950404-09-4
Library of Congress record available
at https://lccn.loc.gov/2021952092

Printed in the United States of America
Cover and book design by N. Putens
Author photo by Stephen Maturen
Cover artwork by Rina Yoon, *Earthbody-24*,
photopolymer gravure, 24 × 35 in. © Rina Yoon
www.rinayoon.com | #rinayoonart

CONTENTS

"What the current time demands is a genuine reckoning with ourselves as the agents of mass extinction…we need to keep faith with death and in so doing to own up to the reality of the world that we are ushering in."

THOM VAN DOOREN AND DEBORAH ROSE, "Keeping Faith with Death" presented at *Dangerous Ideas in Zoology*

"Master Of The Hunt, why am i not feeding, not being fed?"

LUCILLE CLIFTON

ANIMAL AFTERLIFE

magpie

My grandfather's lions want to sleep beside him.

If you let one close, the rest get jealous and make a racket,
whining and pawing at the low bed, they stick their noses
in his stretched, open-mouthed face, wake him up.

He hates them, though the more they appear
the less he rages—he thinks they will eat him.
He has resigned himself to that.

I don't think that's it, I say, the footpads of my fat, mangy lion
slapping the ground behind me. *They only want to be noticed.*

He takes a year to make an inscrutable mark on a piece of paper.

I take his plate to the kitchen, scape off the bite-sized pieces of omelet.

My grandfather is going to die in a different language than he was born.
My mother thinks that's the trouble, he doesn't have a vocabulary for death, never saw it—
but then none of us have. In America, we wait for death like the new high school principal.

I don't know if grief comes from instinct or a disassociation from it.
I heard when an elephant dies, magpies begin to follow its family around.

They rest together sometimes in the graveyards, cry insistent, wordless songs.

raising animals

Some children are raised by wolves.
We couldn't find our words
so we ran to the woods

and watched.

Feral children think they want to be farmers
want to keep horses, goats, maybe a few stray alpacas.
But the want is only to be near animals, to not talk. They
think in languages that do away with the terrible need
for letters, often, for sound. Never a dreamer

you were a kind of farmer—a rancher, once. That night
so childish, I asked for a story to bend the time, and after a pause
playing with where the ends of our hair met on the pillow
so similar in color and texture it was impossible to know
who you touched, who you wrapped around the other—
you told me how the best thing
you've ever gotten in the mail
was a box of baby ducks—soft, small, peeping.
You raised them up for a year and then
rounded them up—took them one by one away.
Somehow *they knew* you said *especially the last*—
you made duck confit out of their little bodies
but something went wrong, and the meat was too tough
gamey and difficult to eat. A good lesson. You were so good

at being human, you knew how to raise an animal
love in your hands when you fed them
love in your hands when you broke their necks.
You were never for a second out of love
so tender every time.

albatross

to have a name synonymous with burden
aching weight around your neck

weight to the wind wings
like my arms outstretched showing you *this*

big if I could be any animal I would be that one
beautiful-eyed big-bodied I'd run off a cliff

and never land
weeks above sea a

part of blue worlds between languages
arms outstretched forever because I would be always

lifted—
maybe

drowning and flying are the same thing really
apart from the comprehensible world

I'd like to live the life of a thing
not its meaning

binturong

(bearcat)

shiver against my snout when the wind
lifts my whiskers / I press them in close
no distractions
I walk the trees and leave myself everywhere
here has been a binturong / buttery self
here has been me and the cloud
of me / I am layers of self / muscle and bone
skin and fur and tufts— shadow and scent
to climb along a vine you need four paws and a tail
I am unafraid
except sometimes / reality / quivers
I shake my tail at it / I shake the hairs
back and forth in the dark / I sway
rhythm of body / air / body / tree
the world moves with me
until it is right / a body can be stronger than a soul
I know every muscle down to my gut / the force of its flex
I don't know how to kill
my work is balance
to hold
feel the shift of a hair on my built neck
to sway

black rhino

there's no sound
so beautiful as my footfall
in the dark / sound of myself / alone
milky light hits my tusk / the only touch
I permit / when I stand near the rocks
I am a rock
the earth and I
steady circle onward / I've never
hit anyone / never / committed violence
against my own species / sitting here
Christmas music blasting / little blonde
children running into my legs
I would like / the joy
of solitude / not the wanting
of your hand close enough to touch wine
in your parent's living room / sliding
home on the ice / there's no creature
more violent to itself than me / if I saw a reflection
I would paw the black dirt / white light
tuck my armored chin I'd
charge

blackburn's sphinx moth

the first me
was suspended life
underground I waited
with the white things the eyeless things
then I was many legs
rippling body of a being without hardness
I moved along green stems
unaware of poison unaware of wasps
that would make homes of me
now / I am a black thing
and I do not know / at what single point
I changed save the one
time of nothingness and pain
of awaking / struggling to breathe
as if someone drew a thread of molten iron through my body
my soul hung on it for a breath outside my lips
I had to retch for it
now here I am / hello / a new thing
overnight I got hard
over many nights I'm told / but I have no way of knowing
I miss being soft in the world
my time as a kitten in a basket / how I imagine myself
helpless mewing heat leaving my body so fast
most could never survive
no / most do not
but here I am a thousand years old
so rare most think I do not exist / that I do not eat
are all changed things forever broken?
I fly now I anoint my lips with honey

kākāpō

(green ground parrot)

this is what good feels like
hunger in the dark / / slow the body down / until / little is given / little
needed / life /is / so / long / I wait for the rimu tree to fruit / mine
is a body of green shadows I hold myself still
until night eyes dilate then blink / / I wait
for the rimu tree to fruit I will never again be able to sleep
beside someone / they're in the bed / they're
out of the bed / it goes on like that / on / and on / on / and / on / I'm
awake in the dark forever I love the sweet smell of myself
everywhere I go I am me I am remembered / I wait
for the rimu tree to fruit / hunger makes it easier to see
every minute not eating is time doing something I've
seen big bodies and they are beautiful and
I hate them I avoid parrots like
me when no one is watching / I hold
a leaf with my foot and strip with my beak / I leave behind
the bones / I am waiting for the rimu tree to fruit
the men will dig holes and *boom boom* sometimes *skraark*
tonight I watched a fat woman put sour cream
on top of cheese on top of meat / white / rice
like someone hit me / I was better than her
I shook my green feathers / I dragged my tail across the floor like a god

northern hairy-nosed wombat

the taste of golden beard grass
at midnight / almost like lemons / black speargrass
slightly bitter / I push my nose into the earth
let my mouth take in small bursts of dirt
there is nothing ground cannot
give / if I paw down
roots contain the sweetest break
water in a plant / oasis / I smell the night
like catching your ghost on my pillowcase
smells of animals and flowers something I can't
put a claw on / when the wild dogs begin to bark
I run through the dirt / my paws wide
when I find a slope I dig
prying open the earth
here are the things I am willing to give:
my back / the slope of my ass
the things / we trade / to save our hearts
our soft faces / our brains / yes
there are scars
but what pain you can endure
when you yourself choose
the exchange / the barking
forward
I dig / teeth / always
forward

pe'epe'emaka'ole

(no-eyed big-eyed wolf spider)

for so long I carried you in my mouth / the world
felt warm for you thick of life close to fire
I felt every breathing thing like a kind
of touching / inside my body changed
I will hold you for a year
I feel the turn / without eyes
we are the only ones who really know beauty
it's the fit of your teeth notched
in the hairs on my back / lock / I know this pressure
my fangs pressing into a body / that moment of puncture & break
each of your small bodies an atonement may you never know violence
once someone asked what I thought about the word
mother / holding her brown hands on the couch / tracing the thought of love
over and over until it could be true / how we teach ourselves
pain / your bodies like pearled onions
my body like a kind of airplane
elephant in the places the Earth is made
where it breaks

nepalese tiger

night is new for me
I miss the sun's fingerpads
thrumming the skin over my heart
I hate that I can't go to our co-op
the Wedge is so expensive and their salads are shit
we've had so many iterations
versions of me
ate versions of you got a little addicted to your gristly taste
you got stuck between my teeth I kind of liked it
so you put a mask on the back of your head
until I realized you couldn't actually see me
you liked to tack me up on display
just parts of me, I
miss the sunlight running across my breasts
I've never been afraid of your bite
it's your hands always on the move
to a goal I don't understand
I am stronger than you
every inch and tooth
a more terrible god
but your skinny two legs
your gaunt face always a little under-nourished
so God-like you have made me different
animal night-being / moon-touched / dark-
or maybe light-itself what-is-not-black
inside a shadow
what
if you don't see
you might forget
or at least / love of my life /
leave alone

black-footed ferret

they thought we all died we just
went underground you can feel daylight
like dust in your fur
I bought my home with blood I was so young starving
my body the space between bones
all day I stood in the shadows / watching them
build their little cities watched them be with each other
as if they liked it / moonlight / I slipped into their den like water
the first never saw it coming
the others ran / they ran / ran / they run
maybe some are still running I only took
what I needed I can't always tell
the difference between kindness and cruelty
it's a question of time people's faces all look the same
when I stand in the den
their bodies (soon my body) pulse slow
with a sleeping breath their arms hold each other
their eyelids twitch
it is the quietest moment in the world
it lasts a hundred years

dwarf crocodile

I was born in my mother's mouth
she broke my world open gently / gnashing / I curled
nose to tail the softest pink I lay on her tongue
and slid between her incisors into the warm hold of water
those teeth white pillars framing my grand entrance
I arrived with style in the dominion of big things
I was a golden child
in the nest of leaves I moved fast
every leg a million paces a minute
to keep up / with her single / slow move
one foot
next foot
crickets were half the length of my body
I stalked them through the grasses
the way I saw my mother
grab hold of a struggling body
thrashing and crushing back
and forth with all my
slight might
I know no truths
about childhood except
I was small / the armor plating on my neck
soft enough to hold a fingerprint
I practiced relentlessly
at being a giant

panamanian night monkey

you were known to me before I caught you in the branches
the smell of your hands like rain I wanted so badly
to touch your fur / press my fingers deep down to the heat of your skin
I have never been very good at boundaries
would you have known I loved you more if I met you at Pat's Tap and left?
my world is this kind of gray and that kind / but you are a brightness
bending leaves inside your closed hand / bringing the thin veins
to your mouth / when we have a child
I want you to carry her the world and the world's
strong arms / we will never be alone
in the trees / moons and moons / above us
in the crests of our nails

aye-aye

no one knows how impossibly gentle
I am in the night my white hairs raised
soft in the slow Madagascar wind
the world is black and the night will go on
forever / I hold my ring finger high tap
tap tap / listen / love in an ant six legs pulsing
for the hunger of the colony someone else's meal
how I miss the self-assurance of friendship knowing
someone's thoughts like you dreamt them
do you know what it is to be hated?
I am love / in the night up a tree
I'm blind but my eyes are wide it's easy
to fill a bed even repeatedly even hated
maybe especially / I hold the world in tree
I carve it of ants there's my love
to draw out / to reach inside

Speak/Sea

All that comes to pass on the fertile earth, we know it all.
—spoken by the Sirens, *The Odyssey*

In the end, your body always finds the surface line.
Water/body/sky. Everything tinging blue.

Red saltwater and air make a body—just a sea
with a firmer edge

inside all storm & wave.

*

To ease a body into water is to know that body
it moves the mass of itself aside, feels all

these fishy movements, pushings of soft

fullness—

as though every edge of skin
were pressed by a billion, trillion fingertips.

Standing, everything cleaves to the body heavy with the water that will not let go.

*

To test the fatness of a body, students in a Christian college
were dunked into bathtubs and the displaced water measured

to determine whether they would be allowed to stay.

Standing up in the tub, the heat from their faces a dry contrast
to the cold water sloshing against the ridge of fibula at their ankles.

*

The Siren of Canosa sang to Persephone, wrapped words in her mouth like ropes—

Here, the human body prepared for the underworld.
Here, statue of a cannibal god pulling you down.

*

After Orpheus, I became obsessed with teaching a man I met how to swim.

We both grew up surrounded by water but his was a neglected childhood
and sometimes violent.

I would fall asleep imagining lesson plans,
how I might run my hands along his back

feel his freckled skin through all that wet, and
pull him throat-to-sky. Compare how it was to fall
asleep (in love), like you give up gripping your body
let loose every spasming muscle, accept your full weight

and in that act of trust—
transformation.

To my knowledge he still does not know
how to swim.

*

Using the bodies of pigs, a group of Canadian scientists determined it takes 90 days for a body to break down in the ocean, the feet will naturally separate and may float for some time depending on the material in its shoes.

*

Of all the human bodies
remaining in the world

a third rest at sea.
Actually, no one knows how many

because they only last
90 days.

*

For scientists to know about the feet,
some of the pigs must have been wearing sneakers. Others maybe high heels.

*

I've never been afraid of drowning—

I am afraid of being found terrifying, impossible to understand,
afraid that when I open my mouth to speak

the thing to come out of my body will be the sound of a bell,
the crush of water as a wave folds.

It happens a hundred times a day
the long pause as if with time my voice would make meaning.

*

In Euripides's *Helen*
she is copied in two,

the true Helen whisked away to Egypt
while her double stumbles through kidnap/war/ravage.

When she learns of so many deaths, Real Helen
cries *What muse shall I approach with tears or songs...?*

in the end,
she speaks to the Sirens.

*

Every mammal on Earth can swim if placed in the water with two exceptions: the giraffe
(certain computer simulations say they *could*)

and great apes. Great apes can swim, but they must be taught by another great ape.

*

We know this because they forced

a bat to swim until it died of exhaustion. Those paper thin wings
doing what they could, but not what they should.

There is an awful high cost to illustrating a point.

*

Sylvia Plath wrote about sirens
with her mind split. As have so many ill

femmes everyone wanted to fuck.
We like to be near the sea. Maybe the Sirens sang

many kinds of songs, but all anyone listened to
was their own name. It is nice to have a voice,

we repeat ourselves with pouted lips
because that is what is heard.

*

Some think the word *siren* came from
σειρά meaning cord

and εἴρω
to join, to fasten

so they are the great entanglers. They lift
salt-wet mouths to the light and speak in braids.

*

Helen, of course,
called sirens *virgins*.

*

The Siren of Canosa was half woman
half bird. As were her sisters.

Often, they are confused with fish.
In the fifteenth century *Myrrour of Worlde*:

They be called seraynes or
mermaydens. The *Noble lyfe Bestes* states

Syrene, the mermayde, is a dedely beste
that bringeth a man gladly to dethe.

I cannot trace the origin
of this confusion.

*

You can see a siren's body in the Peabody Museum
of archaeology and ethnography

though it is actually
half the body of a small monkey, eyes lidless

peeling

half the body of large fish
mummified in the way human hands learned to do

with bodies real and imagined.

*

When the Argonauts sailed, Orpheus drowned out the Siren song with his voice.

Some say if the Sirens failed to entrance they died, maybe by suicide.

I don't believe it. I prefer the earlier myths
that give these winged women a song not to death

but of death, of the road home.
What's falling but another metamorphosis

Persephone in her quiet kingdom

yellow hair like flickering light
luminous through the next world outside the known.

*

Sometimes I see you still in the *Argo*
sails thundering the sea wind—

your brown hair so like my own.

How you ruffle my long feathers,
make me shift my tail.

I see you, but I promise,
I do not speak.

trouble

Mangatambo hita, miseho tsy tsara
if [the aye-aye] is seen, there will be trouble

the history of the world is a history of hunger
fear is a kind of appetite

I hold a branch four fingers / curled round
thumb on the other side

it's almost a pulling / moving through the night-
trees / banner / tail / a balance &

my flag / some will kill me if they see me
cut my tail from my body

separate me and string me up miles between as if
luck could be tricked by distance

some will eat me drag me to the center of the village
gather children around me

hit / maybe ridicule them / until they cry as if luck
could be tricked by sadness

some will see me in the forest building my nest of leafed
branches / and do nothing

for they are in my home / as if even bad luck
must live somewhere in peace

The Fly

Childhood story: Chandragupta Maurya gave up his kingdom to die naked in a forest

Chandra from the Sanskrit word for moon but maybe also simply "shining" / *gupta* maybe from *goytri* for protector / *Mauyra* from Morya Gosavi, famous because he so loved the elephant-headed god Ganesha who both removes obstacles and puts them into place / so in some sense he was a devoted protector of the moon / or devoted and like the moon, protector from the dark / or like the moon devoted and thus protected

He became a Jain—or was already a Jain—and so would have worn a loosely-woven cloth over his mouth and nostrils a simple broom of twigs to brush / brush / brush the ground in front of his feet before each / step because life exists everywhere and we so thoughtlessly eat / it

I once knew a young nun who only walked on pavement to avoid killing the worlds of creatures between blades of grass (something here always struck me as a poor calculation of harm: the laying of pavement > the impact of a foot)

Something I like: that each footstep would atone itself / Some other things I like: the microcosm of an ant holding aloft a drop of dew, a burrowing beetle kicking boulders of dirt behind lean black legs, bamboo forest of inch-high grasses shifting around an elephant of a toad

I have been accused of being an unforgiving person. But I am not really interested in forgiveness. A man I know works to put protection in place for animals in factory farms / on the weekend he consensually hogties women and they call him *Master*… / my family in India always says "sorry" like there's no word for it in Oriya / always "sorry sorry sorry" in triplicate / in song to comfort more than erase

Karma is not a law of justice / the word just means this: *action* / so here is your karmic life / your life of making. What's next?

Another man I knew once visited the land belonging to his great grandmother / where she once lived / like all her family / as slaves and it was rural and just tall grass blowing blue sky / silence / he went next to Kara Walker's *A Subtlety, or the Marvelous Sugar Baby* / threw up in the doorway / never walked in

And isn't that it,   what   in place of forgiveness
do we bring to the dead?   Violence negates closure.   Forgive forgive to
move on / they say / it / is / not / enough / justice is never done. Generous children's story: that stories end.

Our world is on fire / everything you want to save / will consume you

Depicted surrounded by flames Shiva is commonly known as the "cosmic destroyer" ask any yoga student / anyone with an *om* tattoo / and yes but also / he dances the planets into their orbits, light into life / his right hand plays the drum that holds the universe in time / also *shivoham* / may I be part of Shiva / *shivoham* / I am Shiva / *shivoham* / The Billsful One   .

At a party last night a man hit / my shoulder / I was confused for a minute but he held up his hand with a little black speck on it, legs curled into each other / so common / to have violence performed for your benefit

Snakes & Lions

keep appearing in my tarot deck but it might be that I am thinking about them so I see them. I am writing a book about a dead glacier in yet another icy climate but from my desk I can (maybe) see the thinnest glow of a living glacier in the mountains beyond the mountains within the mountains. The sea has crept a long way to lap at these pebbles, the edge of the empty factory that slaps metal with thunderous midnight sounds while I am restless dreaming of the sex I am not having.

The colors: black, blue, violent green life pushing between the rocks. Inside my great aunt's mouth it is red, red inside her nose, on her neck.

I did not think people could suffer like that in the twenty-first century, my mother says and I practice not dissociating into word-groups, assuming. I try to hear each word of her sentence as if it were a series of impenetrable sounds.

Downstairs from her son, in a concrete rectangular house I visited in the dark as a child, I remember the walls so high, topped with broken glass bottles for the birds or the monkeys or the people that might as well be birds or monkeys, my great aunt's body began to rot from the inside out. Her children did not speak with each other—*I don't know, maybe over property*—no one noticed pain make its nest of knives and stones in her wooden bed. Pain I can imagine from the botched de-intubation that retched my insides outside my body, the taste of rotting potatoes in my mouth for weeks—our mind enters a new space when an inhale doesn't drag air. *If you saw her you would be afraid. It would scar a child.*

I don't know that pain has changed in the twenty-first century. In a book I read, a prehistoric woman in a bog is ritually tortured and killed, but I looked it up and archaeologists now believe the horrible breaking of bones, the puncture marks and ripped skin were the inevitable result of the living dirt moving its insides around, no human effort, just Earth. Sometimes I think everything that has ever existed still exists.

But not glaciers. Their time is ending. My grandfather made all our lives. Brought us to America—let me leave it as his body and his mind slowly atrophy, sometimes I pretend I can understand the sounds he makes as language and I feel both cruel and saintly. My father's middle sister has surpassed all expectations and continues to live in 2020. I am writing a book about endangered animals, imagining their voices talking to me or me talking in their voices. Everything that exists has never existed before. I find myself repeating a saying a lot about all sorts of things and feeling the meaning leave, leave completely: *slipping through the cracks.*

The King of Swords is often depicted as both a lion and snake. Lions traditionally symbolize royalty because men are blown over by grandiosity, but the male lion is a sleepy demigod. The snake is an animal of authority. It has peeled its own skin off, it can swallow an uncracked egg and survive for a month, it coils in on itself and soaks in the sun like a stone.

Aren't all poems supposed to be about desire? I feel none of it. I lock eyes with a person and all I feel is startled. Like looking into the center of this fjord, in the miles below the surface waters, what would swallow me whole? In someone else's stomach, are you still alone?

Glass complex

Like all things
the problem arose

from too little light.

She lived a life of intentional delicates
knees small orbs of bone

jutting out from skin

you could tear
with a fingernail.

Like water,
the sun brought illness

she walked along the castle halls

in the middle.

*

To swallow a piano
takes a little time.

She was a methodical child:
string by string, key by key,

it grew surprisingly filling.
Three keys in and she thought

a glass orchestra might fit down her throat,
but by the first leg she knew it could only be

the piano
twirling around her gut

making the most beautiful
tones as she walked

left / right *ding* /
ding almost another voice.

*

All this comes to light
when she reaches my age

described in the program notes
as the "delicate age" or sometimes "gentle age."

Age of many things. I do not think
gentle.

*

It was not a secret she tried to keep,

her body not broken
but holding within itself

such glass strings—

my grandmother said a man
traveled a hundred days

a hundred nights to see a famous palace.

When he arrived, the king
placed a lamp in his hands

oil pearled
above the brim.

*Spill a drop
and your head comes off.*

and at the end

when asked,
I saw nothing.

*

It was not
a delusion she invented,

many then believed their bodies

in part infested with new technology. Both a thing

to look through and inside.

How it crept
inside the gut,

spread along the thigh
like a lake

crystalline
with encroaching ice.

A body
no one touches,

that body might be anything.

*

What heartbreak—

when no one discovers
the secret

you are not hiding.
They look at you

then look
away.

*

He forgave
many things,

my one-time-love. Really,

what would a glass piano
sound like?

Encased in glass thin
as eyelashes.

Enquieted music,
almost another voice.

*

In her time, a body broke
easily as a mind

encouraged
away from the sun.

Disease resides
in the network of muted

fragments, luminant dust
visible in a ray

of light

*

In my childhood I loved this story,

Vishnu once ran from
a demon straight into a fleck

of dust, found it was its own world,

a run of birth, marriage, death.
Then he jumped out,

continued
running—

Impossible to know whether the body
chases me, or I chase this body, so forgiving.

*

The most dedicated doctors
held the delusioned,

the imagined
glass men,

and beat them
hard

enough to break
any glass. *Look*, they said, *look*—

*

There was a time before the piano,

she remembered,

days of wildness, life in skin.

She stood in the unbarred
window feeling wave

and wave of wind
stead / unsteady her—

no need

to brace a mind

unaware of its own loss.

snake

sounds like: be quiet.
impossible to know how, legless,
they run like water

faster
than the laws of physics
should permit—yet there they go

I have been looking
for swimming snakes
but it's so possible

I just dreamed
them up in my childhood
we've been having collective dreams

about snakes
for a very long time.
O Great Remover of Innocence

have you ever been more
than silence?

mule song

I was born a foal / could have just been big-eared
appaloosa spots   could have gotten taller

if shadow's proof of a body
I'm ghosted at noon
then in the dark: all self.

Dickinson said   [I]

troubled the ellipse
and the bird fell.
              In my mind

I move in a white dress in my father's attic.
Isn't this a face?

Isn't mine a long-lashed
blink?

Tie the blue rope

below my eyes,   across my neck.

swallow

my voice
hurts still   hoarse

        like a girl's first word

the kind of wildness that's owned.
In the prophetess's mountain *Spákonufell*

life's too rough to feed one more hungering thing
so horses form their own herds
run broad furred flank

to neck to face to wild unending darkness
when the berries pull down the head of a stem
they're cleaved from the mountain—daybreak

springwake and
circled in barbed wire pens, one then one
to break
or slaughter for meat.

I'll never untaste it / maybe it's right—to eat

never a moral act
rarely a conscious thought to close the jaw, force your muscles down
"smooth muscle" autonomous—

I learned actors filming movies take a bite of food   chew
spit it out when the camera turns   you'll never see them swallow

quick   I remember the diving birds

in the field by my childhood home / black glimmer & away
they die in the absence of eating—almost in an instant

such a heavy trade for flight
perpetual consume consume & shout

this body never full   enough

home
a web of sticks

The Thousand Year-Old Woman

*A hero ventures forth from the world of common day into a region
of supernatural wonder: fabulous forces are there encountered and
a decisive victory is won: The hero comes back from this mysterious
adventure with the power to bestow boons on his fellow man.*

—JOSEPH CAMPBELL, *The Hero with a Thousand Faces*

The second time I was in the psych ward / I did not
thrive

a man proposed to me / a woman who wore socks over her hands
long pants / a white turtleneck I remember like a face

followed me around when I left my single room for / the phone / waiting
to call my new perfect, tall, white boyfriend

who visited almost every day / who looked like every part of his body
was weeping / weeping

the pastor likes you / she loved him, that was obvious
(if the insane can love) / *did you know? The pastor / likes you.*

immigrants / immigrants everywhere and if / I had heart to spare
it would have broken

Think of your life / I was told / *like a Hero's Journey...*
I worked / a whole day / on a puzzle of a Thomas / Kincaid / painting

how lovingly I / built the stone cottage / how I traced my fingers
over / over the single candle in the window / there's no bad art I know, now

I had lost / the ability to really / speak
my hands shook too much to really write

I read a book / about recessive blindness on an island
she's lost the light in her eyes my mother pleaded with my psychiatrist

I pulled my knees / up to my chest / and watched
sure / I nodded / *sure*

she convinced them to let me out for an afternoon
we went to Republic / I watched her drink a beer while I shifted

around a salad how strange the world looked
outside of puzzle form

everyone was walking around / as though someone
waited for them / it would be months before I'd be allowed

to close the bathroom door / the sun hit my skin / like a million
    mosquitoes
I felt the warmth of my own hand

I looked at my mother
all was forgiven / I looked at the bad / waiter

all the sweetest smile for my ghosting face / this world I hated / I opened
    my arms /
I give up / I told the dusted air / *I give in*

"7 of the oldest recipes in history"

small but busy corner of the internet *10 ancient recipes you can try today*
Ancient Roman recipes putting ancient recipes on the plate

3 easy ancient Greek recipes you can make today
recipe isn't an old word, maybe four hundred years

from Latin *recipe* or "take!" but I don't know how it came to mean
bring these things together, this amount, this way

place them in a mouth

some are here for the grotesque the rats double fried
the bread cooked over human shit the pig vulva

aren't we more palatable with our looms of meat
raw fish flash frozen to cull the salmon lice like beauty marks falling off the gill

recipe: really just a chain of events
a spider waiting for a sudden jerk on the thread

maybe it's the web that wants the fly
your home is hungry eat and spin more home

some days I'm overwhelmed by the constant work of eating
unrelenting caretaking of the body like laying bricks over a sheet

pulling hard as it can to lift with the wind

hunger, we pretend, has always felt the same, cured by the same instruction
like every orange in the orchard stings the same sour and sweet against your teeth

not one not any one unique

how to cook during a pandemic

at a certain point: stop.
drink instead copious amounts of water
cup after bitter cup of black coffee until your teeth hurt.

without the constant process of digestion
the body begins to lose some quality of earthliness
how can I describe the elation of emptiness

your insides reaching and collapsing?
like waves, like the elliptical orbit of planets
around a blazing star—don't

do this. I should say that, please stop.
everyone tells me it is about control
but really, honestly, it's just 8 pounds, maybe 12

it's just that I want my pants to be looser
to wear that black dress from that one picture
when I looked, from a certain angle

exactly like anyone.
beautiful doesn't really mean anything, you know,
just a way to punish disorder.

extinction studies

through all this crisis I've been quiet running
sick and wasting then strong as I've ever been
holding onto echoes of news my coffee cup finally giving way

to the crack along its thick side sweating while I nod and make listening sounds
on the phone I found a place to sit alone in the parking lot behind my building
standing like an insect with its many eyes of black windows

an insect in its metamorphosis from factory to subsidized housing
gutted surrounded by the half-constructed condos someone pressed on pause
I don't know who will come to fill them or if they ever will

now that the world succeeded at its big reveal / the strip tease to terrible
I have been trying to say something for a long time
I don't know how to insist that this way we choose to live is what's wrong

not us, not anything inherently bad about being human
the photo I click open often of two men standing on thousands
upon thousands of buffalo skulls with their rifles erect and smiling—just one way

someone told me that when you think you've finally said what you mean
you haven't. Say it three more times. So here I am I am
I am

I am.

a brief history of egyptian gods

When I was younger, I thought
I was Bast living and re-
living many times in an instant.

Reincarnation doesn't always
take that long, like gravity pulls in an ellipses not a circle
when you pick up an orange at the store

hold up your sticky-brilliant planet
ridged and porous, a scar hardening
along the navel you run

your fingers over the skin that sweats
against a too-sharp nail
consider it because you have always considered

everything—
buy no oranges.

I think now maybe I am Nuut, outdated
night sky naked and stretched over the Earth
beautiful and dangerous but

not intentionally either of these things. Not anything at all
just holding myself up, spangled
where I am not the color of space.

how to cut a blood eagle

fairytale world / untouchable
the morning I left my life to hold
a red fruit spherical as the planet
run away from the landlocked state of my dying family
pulled back to the center as it grows / berry pressed
between fingers leaking the thinnest blood / seraphic maybe
a globe of seraphim— / a thousand years ago if I killed a king
they'd punch my lungs through my back to shape wings
release the dogged compulsion for flight
I'd give my body if asked / here
maybe love means let me take you
a part green but mostly black, slick
with factory / water
with a little extra / the gulls catch a hot current
I feel something like my heart leap but mostly I think about the animals
I cannot see the whales in the water the reindeer
in great herds on top of the mountains
the breath from their soft noses like passing fog
like a transit / a moveable warmth
wordless hello/goodbye/hello

The Thousand Year-Old Woman

The child of destiny has to face a long period of obscurity. This is
a time of extreme danger, impediment, or disgrace. He is thrown
inward to his own depths or outward to the unknown; either way,
what he touches is a darkness unexplored. And this is a zone of
unsuspected presences, benign as well as malignant: an angel
appears, a helpful animal, a fisherman, a hunter, crone, or peasant.
— Joseph Campbell, *Hero with a Thousand Faces*

It was by the river / and summertime / so green / and once
they brought in llamas to the gated yard

and we had an hour to let the sun touch our skin like maybe people touch us
watched these confused, quiet animals who also knew

about ropes / stand still / how I sat in the middle
of all these troubled minds and spun them

around my manicured / skinny
fingers / *how* the staff asked *is it you're here?*

I don't know I half-smiled like maybe I just forgot
to pay a parking ticket

I have never been so popular / as I was
the first time around in the psych ward

my roommate had a son she worried over
I know about Asian mothers so how well I listened to her

listened to all of them
I made a best friend

who taught me to look away
when they had us step on the scale first thing in the morning

she and I both
had cats / she taught me about the hospital's secret menu

she ordered ice cream and told me anything you eat in the hospital
doesn't count / she had these thin as nail scars all over her body

we planned to start an Etsy shop selling portraits
of people's pets in unreal colors

my perfect, tall, white boyfriend
visited me every day / sometimes twice / I read / voraciously

I knew it marked a change in my life
I had come to a place part of me would never leave.

I did not
sleep.

One girl did not like me
I offered her a place at my table / the most coveted

she got angry, she thought I was
secret police

I told this to my best friend, laughing, she
pushed a beautiful curl of brown hair out of her eyes

I've been there
she said

I didn't belong there / they didn't let us go outside again
because a man climbed the twenty foot fence

because he also
didn't belong.

moth

the most beautiful boy I ever knew
let me in on the secret ways he was taught to make violence

and I showed him what I was taught /
to survive it

two lessons no one ever asked for but we learned
crammed into the boarding schools of violating and endurance

why
I realized so many years later

women are statistically rarely successful suicides

why maybe
I am so rarely a successful poet

forever interested/attempting the turn away/protect
the way in water you can spin over and over again in a circle

cutting the surface of water
/ breaking back inside / cool sightless quiet world /

escaping forever the wretched
meaning rationality the grabbing hand I learned to anticipate

of what everyone has always wanted of you— and who—

the mouth that's purely decorative

arctic fox

There's nothing so bad about the cold

summer fox with your blotchy coat of browns
I never expected you to stick around

we're both great at brief encounters

the mountain bluffs such good humor
as long as our starving selfishness can grit its teeth

monogamy this and monogamy that

I'd live a life of solitude if it guaranteed I'd live
I heard about a fox

who walked 96 miles a day over ice

island to continent to island to continent
so small in the world to know so much it's imagined

with age we learn how to move outside other people's hunger

here I am with you standing beside me
looking into the yellow eyes of a kit

none of us bound to live more than a year

dhole

demon dog hellhound
and why not? The jungle is big
and I'm not interested in your affection
saved for those that give you what you want
I have my clan of red devils ragged-eared
back-nosed we raise our pups together
let them play with anyone they'd like
sometimes I'm glad for a bad reputation
it's a bit of mystery and plenty of danger
kind of glamorous no one
shows up on your doorstep unannounced
no one asks to borrow what they'll never return
sometimes it is exhausting
staying a step ahead of your ideas
blame for the weather and the ensuing retaliation
at its worst when you kill us and say *just leave it*
our bodies leaking wet white paper towels in the red dirt

exmoor pony

the last wolf in England was run down in 1390
so far south & bloody-pawed

to live on this island is to have made peace with sheep

my wildness
is more a wildish

my uncorrupted spine is no promise

I see my cousins with weight behind or above them so long
they have forgotten what it is to be your body's only rider
how to run the herd into a storm

lighting bodies one body breath a rage of steam

and maybe, yes, I am descended from kept horses
or maybe my shaggy coat's the same as the ancients'
hooves that stomped down on panthers

ran alongside mammoths
captured only in paint on smoky walls
traced by human hands with an awesome reverence
no one ever thought to break

angonoka tortoise

(ploughshare tortoise)

beauty undid me

for so long I was the safest place in the world
I outlived generations

swallowing a single bite of dried bamboo

we fought great battles in early spring
close enough to touch crown to armored leg

I'd push chest against shell

turn or be turned belly to sun
head tucked, arms close

harm was never the point—more like, stay there

for a little
let me do my business

we've always been the most gorgeous islanders

high-arching domes all soft yellow & red
eyes wet black jewels

we are slow walking art shaped by the hand of survival

roaming some manicured lawn of Kentucky bluegrass
our only remaining hope

disfigurement

white-headed vulture

no love like this

buoyed up—unbounded body
hunger thrashed itself out

beauty carved itself clean

I'm only lightness
waiting on the wreckage

life brings upon itself

I shrug my feathers against my head
unadorned, unglorious, un-

stained by what I bend

open my curved mouth to take inside me
take back to warmth, to metamorphosis

to the lightlessness within a life

addax

(white antelope)

heavy-headed, I never moved fast
save the moment I was born wet and sticky
into the sand first taste of dry heat
my mother running her soft nose
under my belly lifting me inches
into the air I pressed my hooves to the ground
it gave a little underneath me I fell back down
pushed knees and back hooves rose
a little higher fell back there has never been
such a need within me my heart beating alone
for the first time beating fast my ears moved
back and forth taking in the sounds
of the unmuffled world what wants to eat you
and where I rose and fell for terrifying minutes
so close to birth and death until I stood
pushed down the need to tremble
to wobble I walked as though
I had been for a hundred years
the mightiest thing under the sun

silky sifaka

(simpona lemur)

phantom angel of the mountains
my body like a bone white languorous
in the trees I feel the day on my face breath
against a smooth and hairless cheek
I can't live in someone's hand
we glide through dappled light rest a moment
finger-deep in the textured back of a rosewood
sunk in the smell of leaves each a perfect green teardrop
in the ever-smaller-shape of our home we are still
never without each other's warmth never without
wide brown eyes for those
who would mow us down cleaving
dread of steel knuckled fingers that split the trunk
take its bloody core far from here from me / everyday home
this forest grows the hole of a heart

orcas of the salish sea

(southern resident killer whales)

because we are so often out of sight,
rumors of our transformations have been greatly exaggerated

wiser minds thought we might be wolves

smooth skin softening to wrinkled pink and furry-
warm to the touch

elongated phalanges shrinking down to knuckle black claws

friction against solidity and dirt
knives at the kind of blood that pools

others called us men

residing in cavernous palaces on the ocean's floor
staffing our domestic needs with eager-whiskered sea lions

or welcoming in your dead to a second life in the blues

how hard it must be
to imagine our bodies entirely sufficient

how we were born into the salty world while our mothers stilled their fins

gliding belly to the light so they could see us first
pushed into the cold and kicking

how we swam for many years in their easy slipstream

the gods we never left and the homes that carried us
decades and generations through our long & braided lives

spotted seahorse

you may think of me as winged

ocean angel / half snake
city dweller

my body

to hold & entangle
hours and days of nothing / learning
the weight of another body

circumference of snout
diameter of ringed eyes

length between the ridges of a belly
you turn and I'll spin

I've always loved best with curiosity

nothing like the thrill

of finding someone's beauty
scales and spines and secret mesmer

revealed like an octopus drifting narrowly upward
lifting all eight arms suddenly the whole horizon

alit with color

cook inlet belugas

water moves a loosening trail
currents and baubles of air catch ice white
the dark like a broken blue pen spreads ink &

light where the paper breaks through

liquid pulling up pockets and curves
where things were straight

duotone landscape / mine

the kind of beauty of a few bright things
the way we've learned to stay warm imitate
the palate of ice

the sort of place you look at for a long time
and let out slow / sounded breath

I wouldn't mind if you came
I wouldn't mind you

why would I

something so colorful & delicate?

whale shark

marokintana many stars

cover my body
so close to yours

my live young, my open mouth—

the sea is a vehicle for light
crossing bright afterimages of wave caught

on my back, stars in a tender galaxy

I move neither fast nor deep
like a metronome my tail goes right / left

I make my work a steady harvest

survey of warm waters
taken into my body, filtered of their smallest beings

released back to the current's bigger mouth

I feel sun fall below the horizon
slight cool of moonlight

the drama of sky given silent echo

when it dips from air
to water holding bodies like a breathless cloud

phoenix petrel

I wasn't named for a firebird

for everlasting life

engulfed reincarnations

but for an island, an atoll

my place of birth and my home of coral

is it rebirth

every time I lean back

from my white egg, its shell pecked

from the inside out, every time a body falls having lost its ghost

for smaller bodies' consummation/consumption/degradation?

You have so much anger at the power the world has over you

can't you be a rock

erode just slowly enough for the coral to grow

all these lives & bodies

replacing what we lose

animal afterlife

is people. I've heard butterflies
remember their lives as caterpillars
but I cannot imagine how

anyone knows this if
deep down somewhere you remember
the hands that kept you living

when you pulled yourself
through a world made of colored shapes
before your eyes unclouded

to take in the gist of letters
the one life with its billion noises
promising only this

gradual erasure.
What strange joy I've known
being made animal on random days

losing language like sometimes
you take a wrong turn and cannot
imagine how to make your way home.

Every dead bird means something to someone.
Warmth is the only way of knowing,
something like God shooting through you

how even buried in a chrysalis
life builds a face
to the sun.

NOTES

The *Blackburn's sphinx moth* was thought extinct until 1984.

Every five years, corresponding with the fruiting of the rimu tree, the male *kākāpō* will begin to construct "bowls" (wide shallow holes) to entice mating partners. Inside the bowls, the kākāpō will make loud, low calls (sometimes described onomatopoeically as "boom" or "shraark"), with the shape of the bowl amplifying the call to potential mating partners.

The *no-eyed big-eyed wolf spider* carries its eggs inside its mouth and its young on its back. The critically endangered spider resides deep in volcanic caves.

The *Nepalese tiger* has recently become nocturnal to avoid run-ins with human beings. The entanglements between humans and tigers have always held great danger for both animals. For some time, humans living close to tigers wore masks on the backs of their heads so approaching tigers would not be able to tell if humans saw them; however, tigers did eventually figure out the ruse, and the practice was abandoned.

Black-footed ferrets live in prairie dog tunnels that have either been abandoned naturally or once housed a colony killed off by ferrets.

Crocodiles, including the *dwarf crocodile*, are carried in their mother's mouth. Despite the myth that reptiles do not raise their young, baby crocodiles will stay with their mother for a year or more.

The Panamanian night monkey forms monogamous bonds, typically giving birth to only one offspring per year. The offspring is carried by the father.

Aye-ayes, the only nocturnal primate, have a very long finger they use to grab at bugs and other snacks inside tree branches. They will tap at branches and listen for echoes to identify the location of insects and grubs.

Speak/Sea:

> Oral Roberts University used a filled bathtub to measure a student's "body mass". If students were deemed too fat, they were asked to take a leave of absence until they achieved a weight the university deemed acceptable.
>
> The Siren of Canosa statues date back to the fourth century BCE. They frequently adorned burial sites and may have been thought to ferry the dead to the afterlife (and also eat men). In later mythology, the psychopomp responsibilities of the siren decreased. They became more monstrous than deified.
>
> Research on the decomposition of pigs used to understand how human bodies decompose at sea (similar in size, gut bacteria, and hairlessness), was published by Simon Fraser University in 2016.
>
> Throughout the 1950s and 1960s, research on whether species could or could not swim resulted in the deaths, by drowning or exhaustion, of most study subjects. More humane research by Anne Dagg and Doug Windsor, published in 1973, confirmed the swimming abilities of 27 land animals under far safer, and more controlled, environments.

Definitions, etymology, and word use are courtesy of the *Oxford English Dictionary*.

So called "Fiji mermaids" were popularized by P.T. Barnum but can still be found in museums around the world. Early taxidermy resulted in surreal shrinking of animal bodies, which may have contributed to the Frankenstein-like creative impulses by early taxidermists to bind animal carcasses together as "mermaids" and "dragons". As the technology of taxidermy improved, most efforts went toward creating realistic replications of animals for natural history museums or private collections.

In some parts of Madagascar, the phrase *"mangatambo hita, miseho tsy tsara"* refers to folkloric traditions which view the aye-aye as a sign of ill fortune or even death. The "fady," or taboo, of the aye-aye are somewhat described in this poem. The fady rarely extends to aye-ayes encountered in their natural habitats outside human communities.

Well-preserved mummies in the bogs of England indicate extreme torture and subsequent execution dating back around 2000 years. Sarah Moss depicts and mocks such an execution in her excellent work, *The Ghost Wall*. However, some contemporary archaeologists suggest the injuries seen on the mummies were the result of natural movements within the complex ecosystem of the bogs, and not inflicted pre-mortem as part of a ritual execution.

Princess Alexandra of Bavaria suffered from the delusion that she had swallowed a glass piano, and any trauma to her body would break the glass and kill her. When glass became a more popular material in Europe (around the 15th–17th centuries), a so-called "glass delusion," in which individuals believed part or all of their body had turned to glass at great peril to their lives, became a recognized disorder. We find references in Robert Burton's *Anatomy of Melancholy*, Miguel de Cervantes's *El licenciado Vidiera*, and René Descartes's *Meditationes de Prima Philosophia*. Some doctors did strike their patients to disprove the delusion, though this was likely far from effective. Delusions often reflect concerns of a particular cultural moment.

"When you troubled the ellipse— / And the Bird fell—" is from Emily Dickinson's poem, "Let Us play Yesterday".

Soil differences, even within the same orchard, can result in different levels of sweetness in oranges and other fruits.

The photograph below was taken in 1892 outside Michigan Carbon Works in Rougeville, Michigan. It is housed in the Burton Historical Collection in the Detroit Public Library. In researching for this book, I frequently encountered European colonialism and settler colonialism as primary factors for species decline. Imposition of European agricultural techniques on various unique environments has had major environmental impact. Wild animals make up an estimated 4% of mammals on Earth today. Of the remaining 96%, 34% are humans and 62% are livestock animals. Unregulated hunting practices, impositions of foreign conceptualizations of the monstrous, and fetishization (horrifically visible in treatment of non-European peoples, as well) have had a devastating and lasting impact. European colonialism coincided with the birth of modern taxonomical categorizations of plants, animals, and human beings. The exploitation of people and nonhuman people was necessary to execute the numerous, devastating, and unresolved crimes of colonialism and its counterpart, capitalism.

Courtesy of the
Burton Historical
Collection, Detroit
Public Library

The *blood eagle* is a (perhaps) imagined style of execution from the Icelandic Sagas in which the lungs are pulled out of brutal incisions made in a person's back to create an illusion of wings. The blood eagle ritual was performed in the Sagas after a regicide and also represented in Ari Aster's *Midsommar*.

It is believed that many *moths* do not have mouths in their final stage of metamorphosis.

A female *arctic fox* released in the Svalbard Islands, Norway, was located 76 days later on Ellesmere Island in Canada. While it is not unusual for foxes to travel great distances, this arctic fox broke all known records for both speed and distance traveled. Not all foxes journey. Research on the Bylot Island foxes from 2008-2009 showed some foxes traveling over 80 miles, and some did not leave their home territory. Mortality rates during infancy are low but rise to 74% during an Arctic fox's first winter, dropping to 32% in subsequent years. High mortality rates in the first year of life are not uncommon in many species. Arctic foxes are monogamous.

Dholes, red dogs, or whistling dogs, can tree a tiger when working as a clan of 12-40 individuals (largely mature females). As they rarely killed livestock and their kills could be easily appropriated for human consumption, some Indian communities welcomed their presence. Though they have not been domesticated, dhole pups have been known to play with domestic dogs. Dholes were heavily persecuted under British colonialism, with bounties of around 25 rupees for each kill. This was due to a false belief by the British that the dholes threatened game hunting animals. This is largely believed to be the reason for their current precarious population status.

Biodiversity in the United Kingdom is among the lowest on the planet. Andy Purvis of London's Natural History Museum stated in 2020, "We have led the world in degrading the natural environment." Wolves and bears were killed off long ago; however, species loss continues, and 40 million birds have disappeared from the UK since 1970. Theories that the *Exmoor pony*, a semi-feral herd in southwest England, are descended from prehistoric wild ponies remain unproven. Written records of the ponies date back to the 11th century.

Due to its stunning domed shell, the *Angonoka tortoise* is one of the most valuable tortoises on the black market. Males will attempt to knock each other on their backs, largely interpreted as a method of establishing dominance.

The *addax*, like other antelopes, is most vulnerable in the moments after its birth. It will learn to stand within minutes of being born.

Rosewood, the preferred home of the *silky silfaka*, is illegal to harvest. However, demand is high for rosewood as high-end building material, particularly prized in luxury furniture. The desire for the resource places disproportionate pressure on financially-drained communities, allowing ghost structures of European colonialism to drive resource extraction, yet also demonize West African and Malagasy communities for their partici-pation in illegal trade. Environmental conservation movements are often positioned as a "Western" construct, yet they are a byproduct of European and settler colonialism and often reinforce the ideology that is directly responsible for the environmental degradation they seek to correct.

Orcas pass down cultural practices within matriarchal pods that are either migratory or resident to a single location. Some biologists even theorize that the category of "orca" describes multiple species. Some myths braid together the orca and wolf as the same animal, able to transform and live in the sea or on land. Other stories describe how the orca transforms into undersea men who govern over drowned human beings, waited on by sea lion servants.

Belugas are notoriously friendly toward humans, even known to play games of catch near the beach or with humans on small boats.

ACKNOWLEDGMENTS

"black rhino" appeared in *SWWIM*.

"Glass Complex" appeared in *Mid-American Review* and was a finalist for the *Black Warrior Review* Poetry Prize.

This book would not exist without the contributions of countless mentors, teachers, friends, and my human and non-human kin.

Many thanks for the support of the Minnesota State Arts Board's Artist Initiative Grant, Kunstnarhuset Messen, and the Loft Mentor Series. A deep thanks to my parents for giving me a place to safely follow curiosity, and to all my grandparents and relations for their wisdom, in particular Sudhansu and Induprava Misra, who have shared with me remarkable grace.

Inexpressible thanks to my sweetest, most brilliant friends and creative co-conspirators, Brianna Flavin, aegor ray, Shelby Dillion, Nick Gettino, Jordyn Taylor, and Asha Stenquist. A great gratitude to the brilliant teachers and advisors I've had over the years, including, among many, Justin Armstrong, Alison Hickey, Dan Chiasson, Frank Bidart, Amy Quan Barry, and Danez Smith.

Thanks to the generosity of Airlie Press, in particular editors Jennifer Reimer, Connie Soper, and Brittney Corrigan, for the opportunity to release this wild book into its natural habitat.

AIRLIE PRESS IS GRATEFUL TO THE FOLLOWING SPONSORS
and individuals, whose contributions provided major support in
funding this and other Airlie Press books of poetry.

Joelle Barrios

Joanie Campf

Jane Comerford

Chip Ettinger

Cecilia Hagan

Quinton Hallett

Dennis Harper

Donna Henderson

Hannah Larabee

John Laurence

Karen McPherson

Alida Rol

Kat Sanchez

OREGON **ARTS**
COMMISSION

Oregon

Community

Foundation

ABOUT THE PUBLISHER

Airlie Press is run by writers. A nonprofit publishing collective, the press is dedicated to producing beautiful and compelling books of poetry. Its mission is to offer a shared-work publishing alternative for writers working in the Pacific Northwest. Airlie Press is supported by book sales, grants, and donations. All funds return to the press for the creation of new books of poetry.

COLOPHON

The poems are set in Minion, a modern adaptation of late Renaissance style printing types. Released in metal type by the British branch of the Monotype Corporation in 1938, its digitized form sets narrow and crisp on the page. The titles are set in Chalet Book. Adapted by House Industries from the original Chalet design by fictional designer Rene Albert Chalet, the more practical book version evokes a familiar swiss-based design.

Printed in Portland, Oregon, USA